GRAPHIC HISTORY

NAT TURNER'S SLAVE REBELLION

by Michael Burgan
Illustrated by Richard Dominguez,
Bob Wiacek, and Charles Barnett III

Consultant:
Theodore C. DeLaney, PhD
Associate Professor of History
Washington and Lee University
Lexington, Virginia

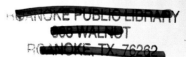

Capstone
press

Mankato, Minnesota

Graphic Library is published by Capstone Press,
151 Good Counsel Drive, P.O. Box 669, Mankato, Minnesota 56002.
www.capstonepress.com

Printed in the United States of America

1 2 3 4 5 6 11 10 09 08 07 06

Library of Congress Cataloging-in-Publication Data
Burgan, Michael.
Nat Turner's slave rebellion / by Michael Burgan; illustrated by Richard Dominguez, Bob Wiacek, and Charles Barnett III.
p. cm.—(Graphic library. Graphic history)
Includes bibliographical references and index.
ISBN-13: 978-0-7368-5490-0 (hardcover)
ISBN-10: 0-7368-5490-8 (hardcover)
1. Turner, Nat, 1800?–1831—Juvenile literature. 2. Southampton Insurrection, 1831—Juvenile literature. 3. Slaves—Virginia—Southampton County—Biography—Juvenile literature. 4. Slave insurrections—Virginia—Southampton County—History—19th century—Juvenile literature. 5. Southampton County (Va.)—History—19th century—Juvenile literature. I. Dominguez, Richard, ill. II. Wiacek, Bob, ill. III. Barnett, Charles, III, ill. IV. Title. V. Series.
F232.S7B87 2006
975.5'5503092—dc22 2005029332

Summary: In graphic novel format, tells the true story of the 1831 Virginia slave rebellion led by slave Nat Turner, who believed he was a prophet.

Art Direction
Bob Lentz

Designer
Thomas Emery

Storyboard Artist
Blake A. Hoena

Production Designer
Kim Brown

Colorist
Sarah Trover

Editor
Christine Peterson

Editor's note: Direct quotations from primary sources are indicated by a yellow background.

Direct quotations appear on the following pages:
Page 21, from a September 1831 article by John Pleasants printed in *The Constitutional Whig*, Richmond, Virginia; page 22, from the Court Records of Southampton County, Virginia, August 31, 1831; page 23, from an article in *The Petersburg Intelligencer*, Petersburg, Virginia, originally printed in November 1831, as published in *The Southampton Slave Revolt of 1831*, by Henry Irving Tragle (New York: Vintage Books, 1973).

TABLE OF CONTENTS

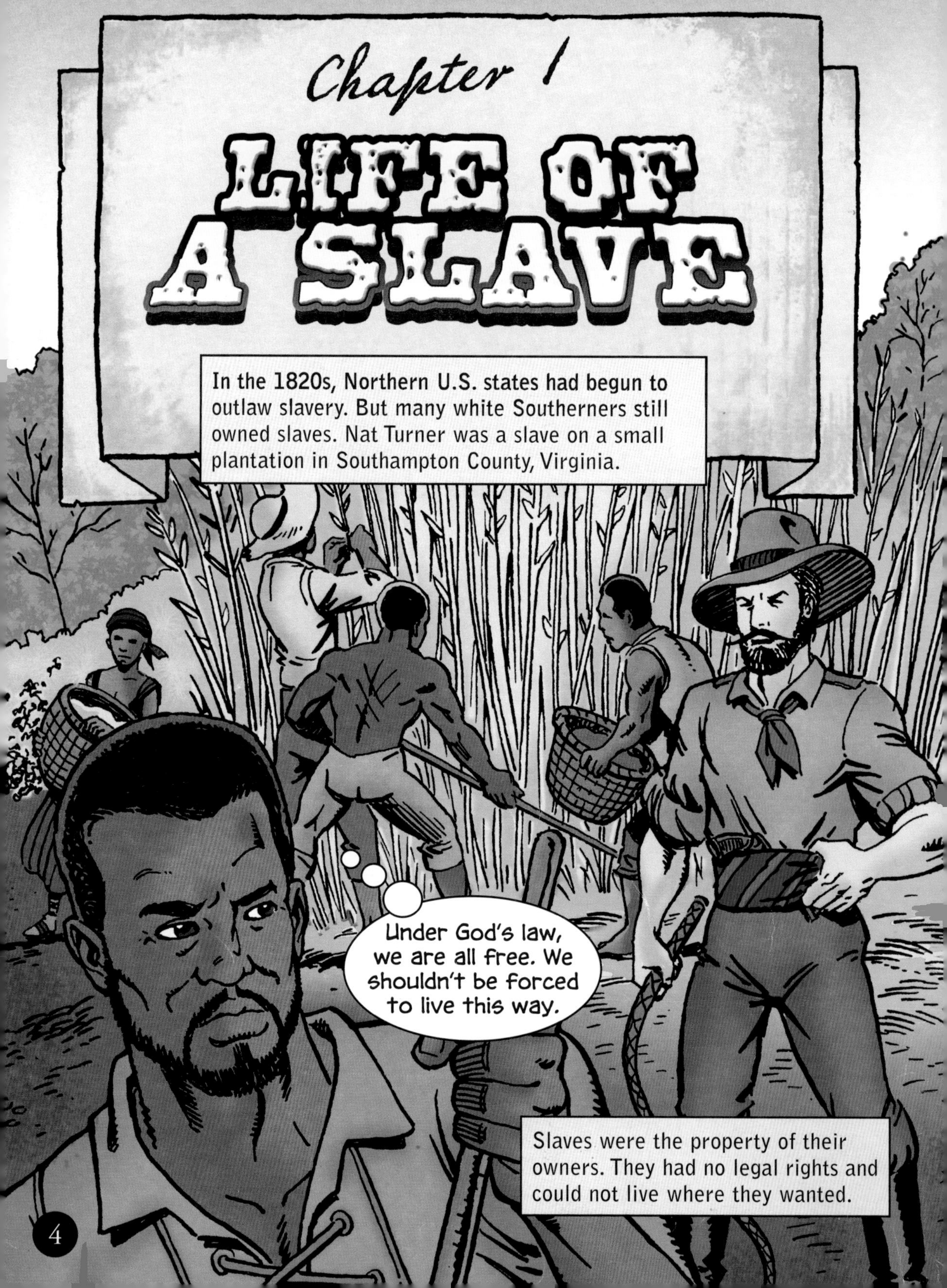
Chapter 1
LIFE OF A SLAVE
In the 1820s, Northern U.S. states had begun to outlaw slavery. But many white Southerners still owned slaves. Nat Turner was a slave on a small plantation in Southampton County, Virginia.
Under God's law, we are all free. We shouldn't be forced to live this way.
Slaves were the property of their owners. They had no legal rights and could not live where they wanted.

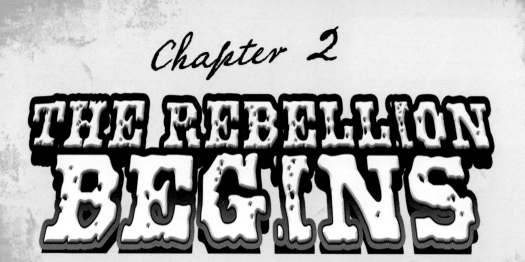

Chapter 2
THE REBELLION BEGINS

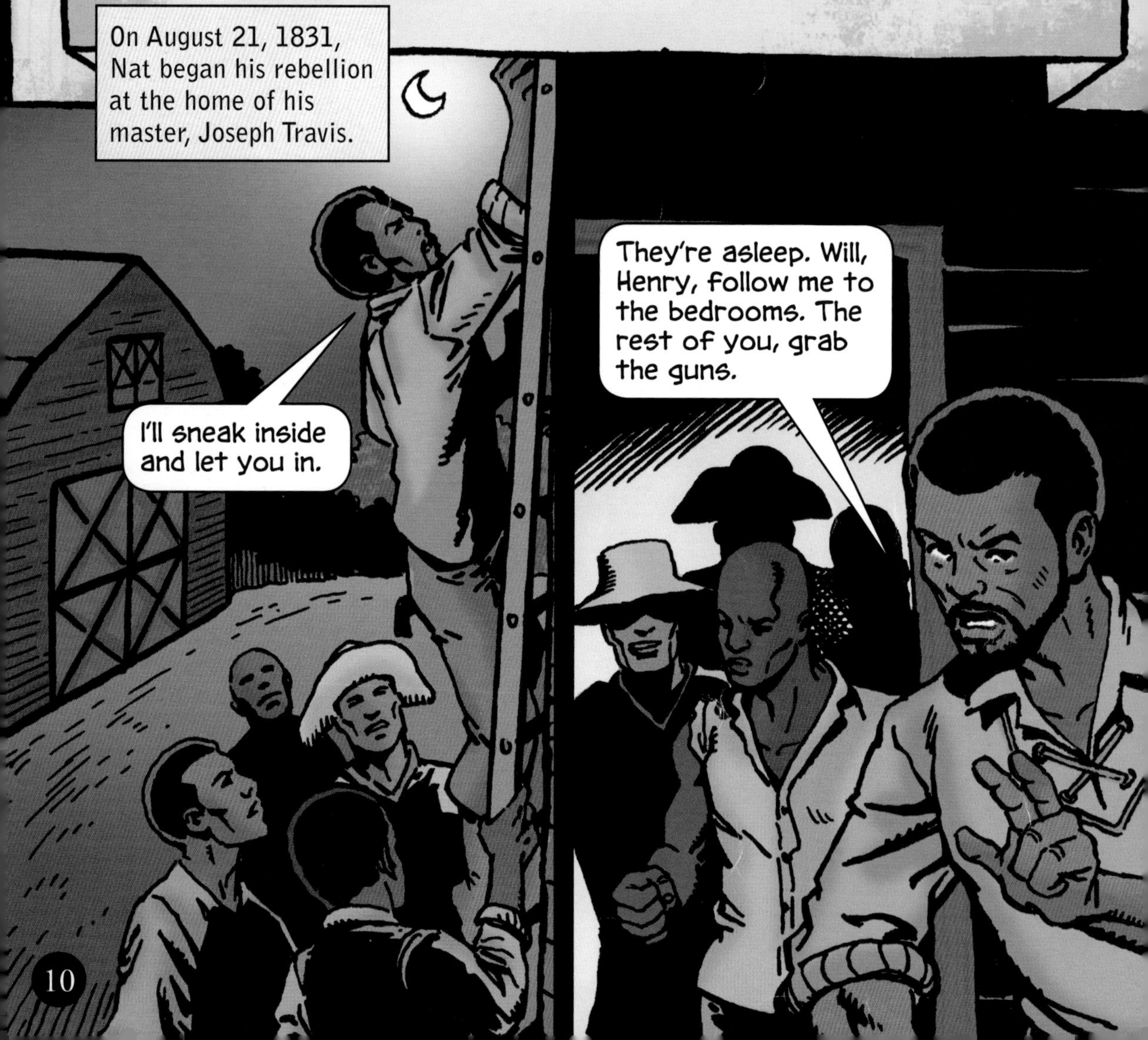

On August 21, 1831, Nat began his rebellion at the home of his master, Joseph Travis.

I'll sneak inside and let you in.

They're asleep. Will, Henry, follow me to the bedrooms. The rest of you, grab the guns.

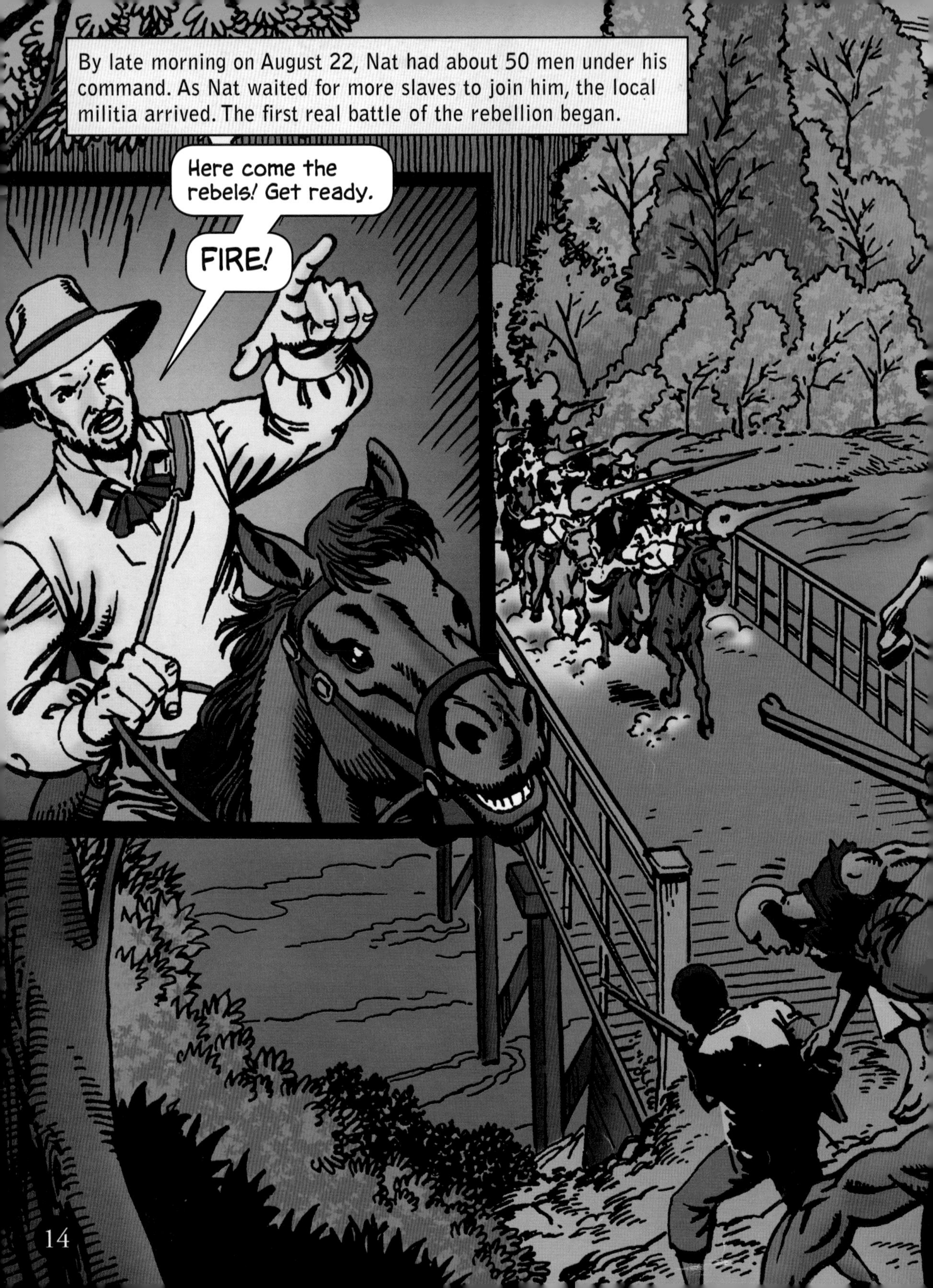
By late morning on August 22, Nat had about 50 men under his command. As Nat waited for more slaves to join him, the local militia arrived. The first real battle of the rebellion began.
Here come the rebels! Get ready.
FIRE!

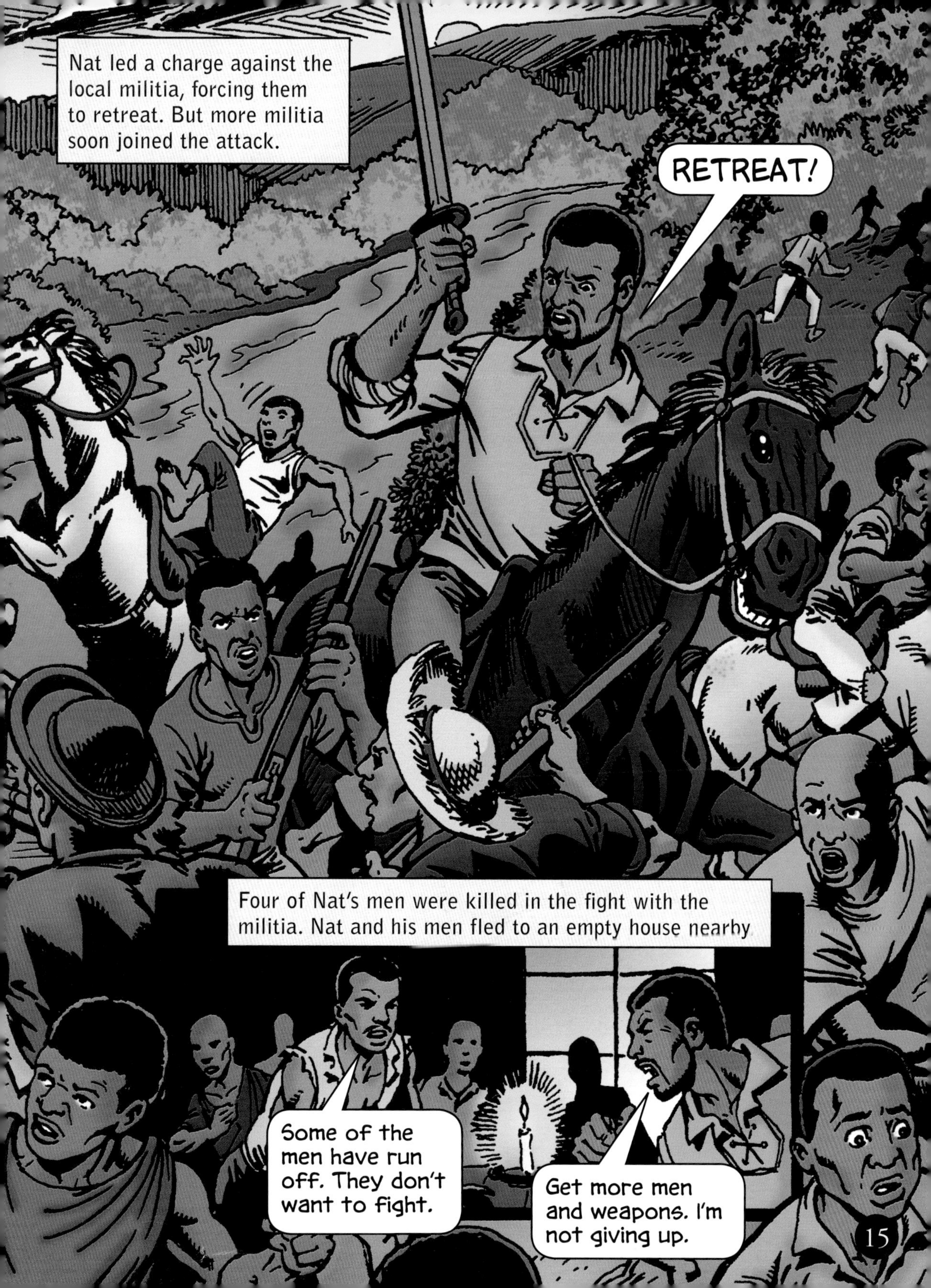

Nat led a charge against the local militia, forcing them to retreat. But more militia soon joined the attack.
RETREAT!
Four of Nat's men were killed in the fight with the militia. Nat and his men fled to an empty house nearby.
Some of the men have run off. They don't want to fight.
Get more men and weapons. I'm not giving up.

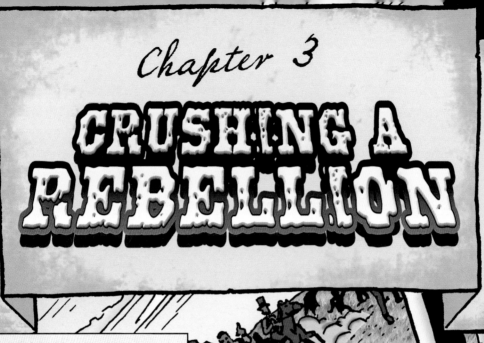

Chapter 3
CRUSHING A REBELLION

On the morning of August 23, Nat still had about 20 men with him. He hoped to find new recruits at the home of Samuel Blunt. Nat wanted to make sure the family was gone.

Samuel, his son Simon, and several other men were hiding in the home.

Go ahead and fire, Hark. See if anyone is there.

Get your guns ready, boys.

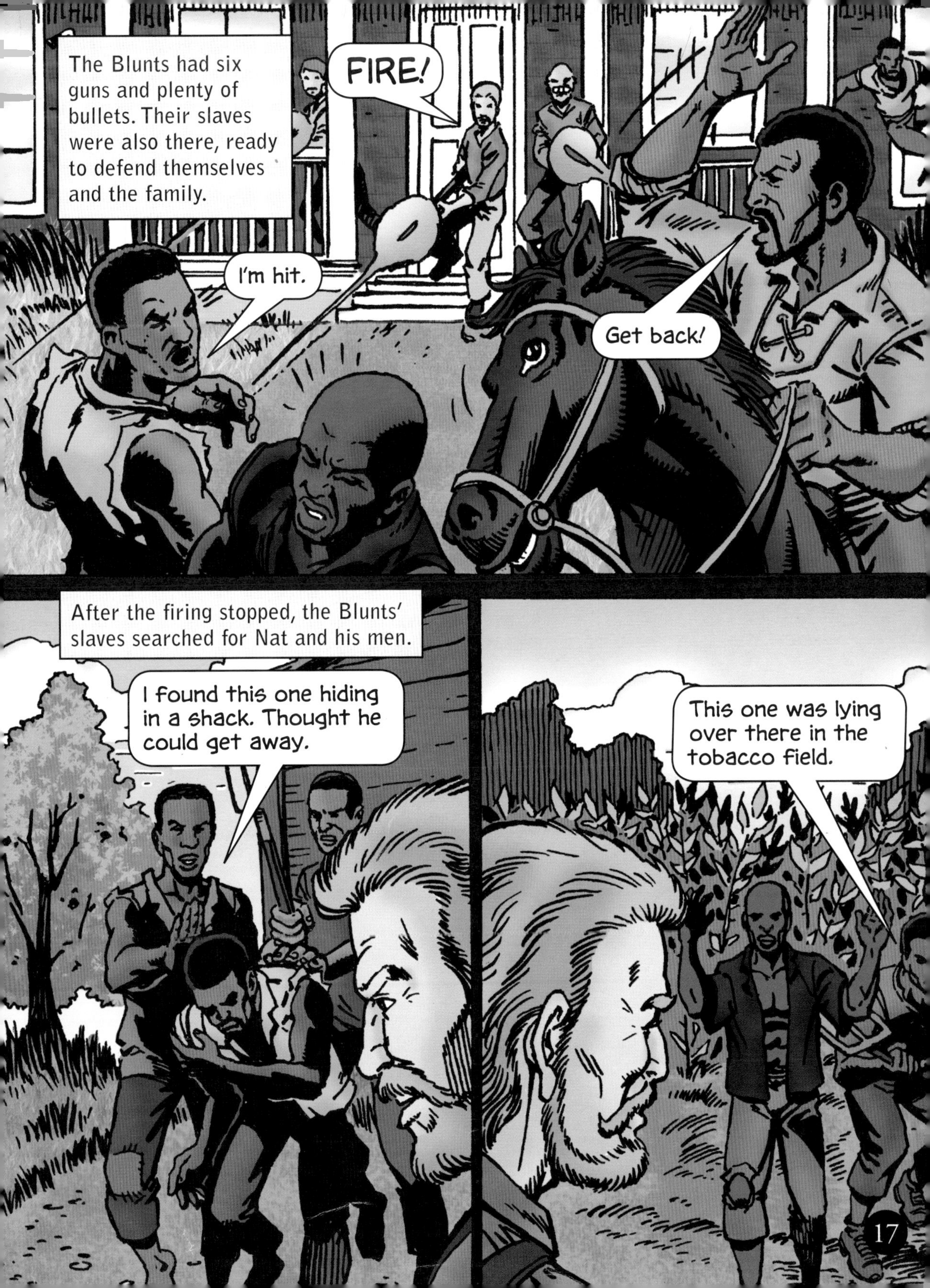
The Blunts had six guns and plenty of bullets. Their slaves were also there, ready to defend themselves and the family.
FIRE!
I'm hit.
Get back!
After the firing stopped, the Blunts' slaves searched for Nat and his men.
I found this one hiding in a shack. Thought he could get away.
This one was lying over there in the tobacco field.

Nat and a small group of slaves escaped from the Blunt's house, but they soon ran into more militia.
It's the rebels. Don't let them get away!
Fire!
Run!

Some of the slaves had fled in one direction, while Nat and a small rebel band went another. That night, Nat still hoped for victory.
You two, go look for Hark.
Two of you go get more recruits.
Meet me at the pond by morning.

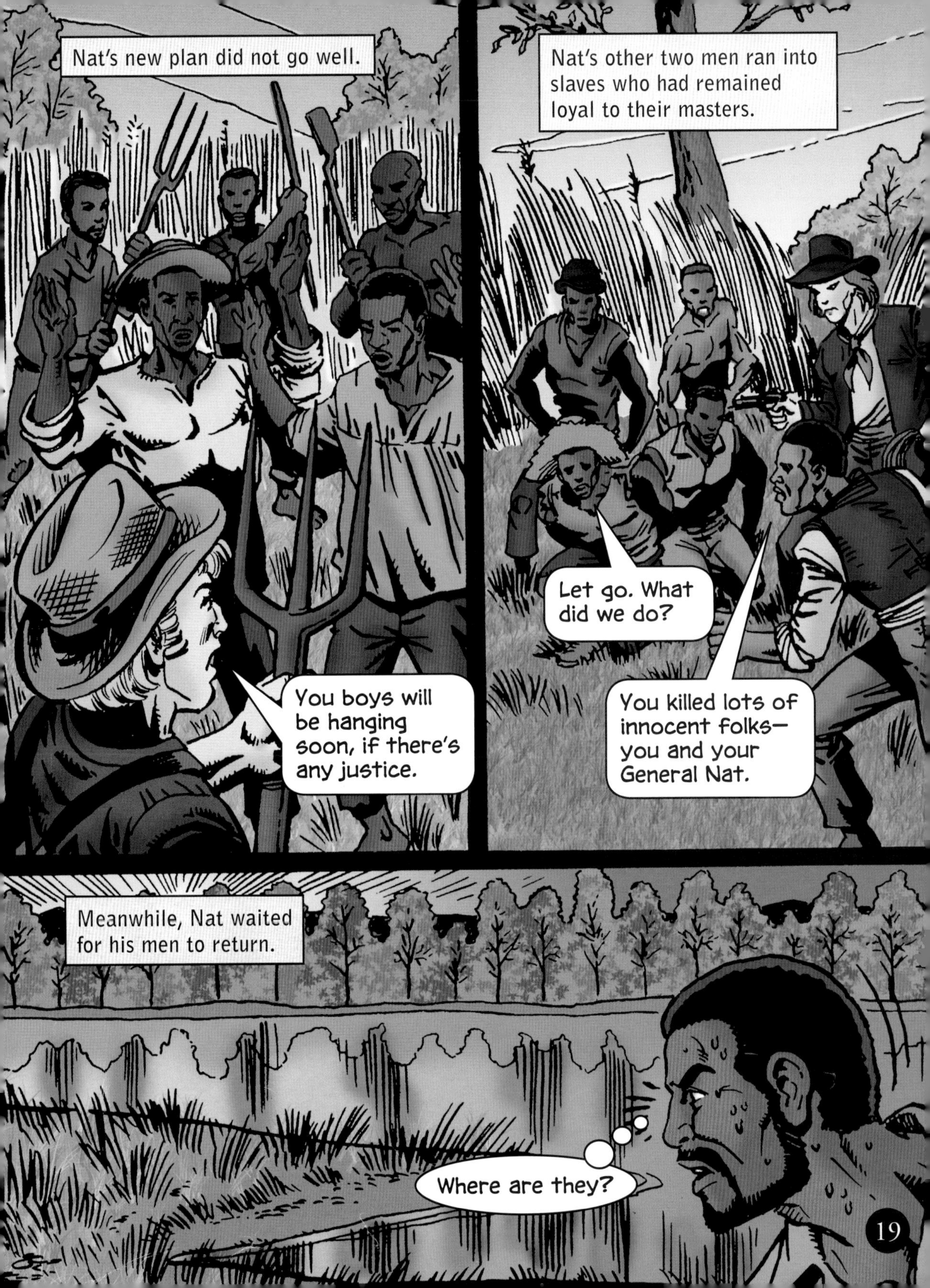

Nat's new plan did not go well.
You boys will be hanging soon, if there's any justice.
Nat's other two men ran into slaves who had remained loyal to their masters.
Let go. What did we do?
You killed lots of innocent folks— you and your General Nat.
Meanwhile, Nat waited for his men to return.
Where are they?

21

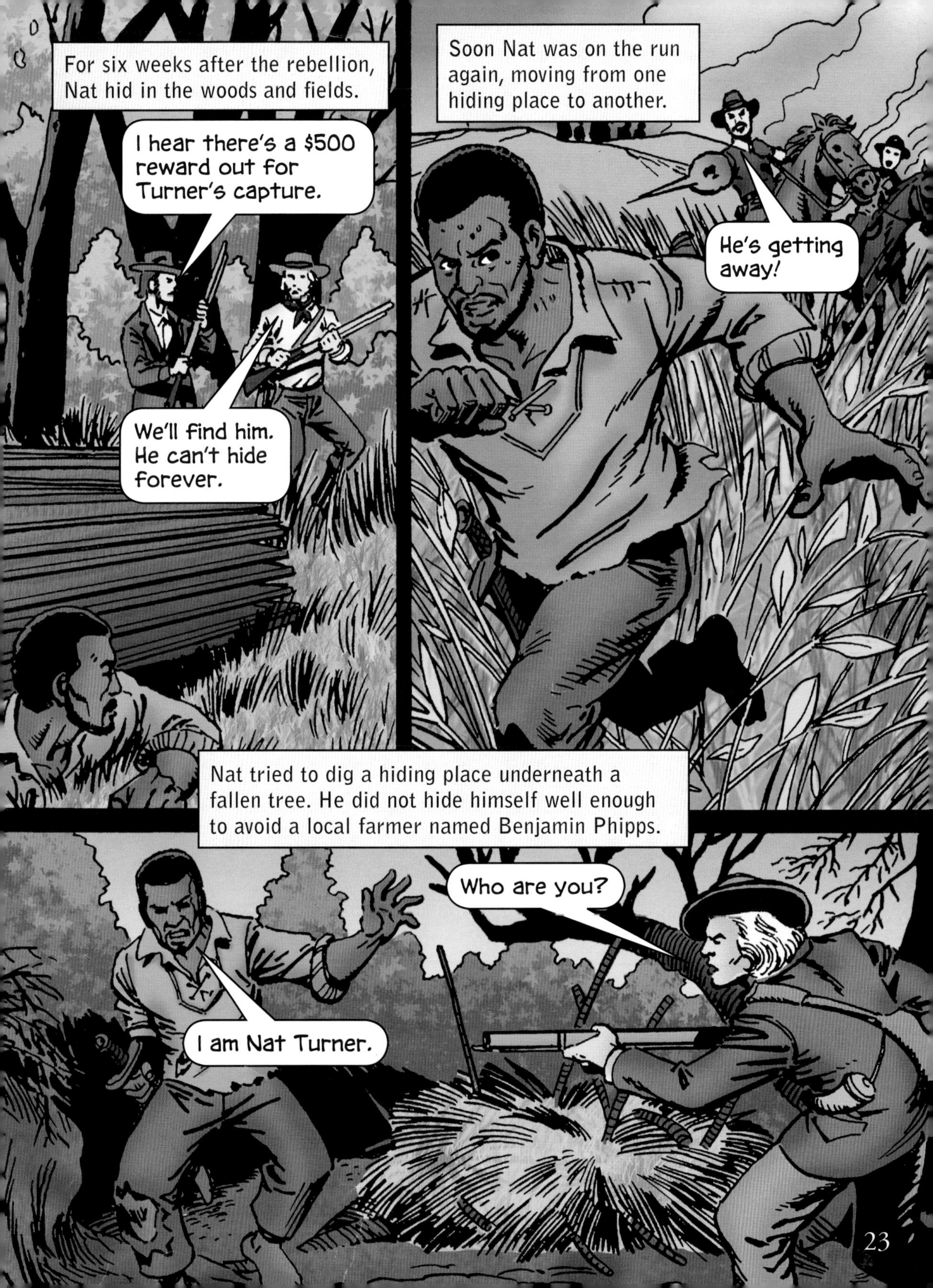
For six weeks after the rebellion, Nat hid in the woods and fields.
I hear there's a $500 reward out for Turner's capture.
We'll find him. He can't hide forever.
Soon Nat was on the run again, moving from one hiding place to another.
He's getting away!
Nat tried to dig a hiding place underneath a fallen tree. He did not hide himself well enough to avoid a local farmer named Benjamin Phipps.
Who are you?
I am Nat Turner.

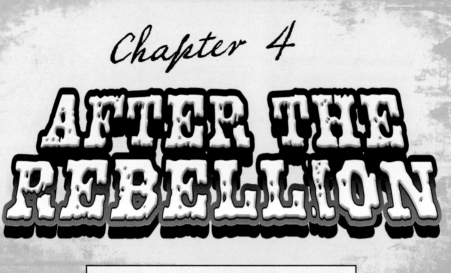

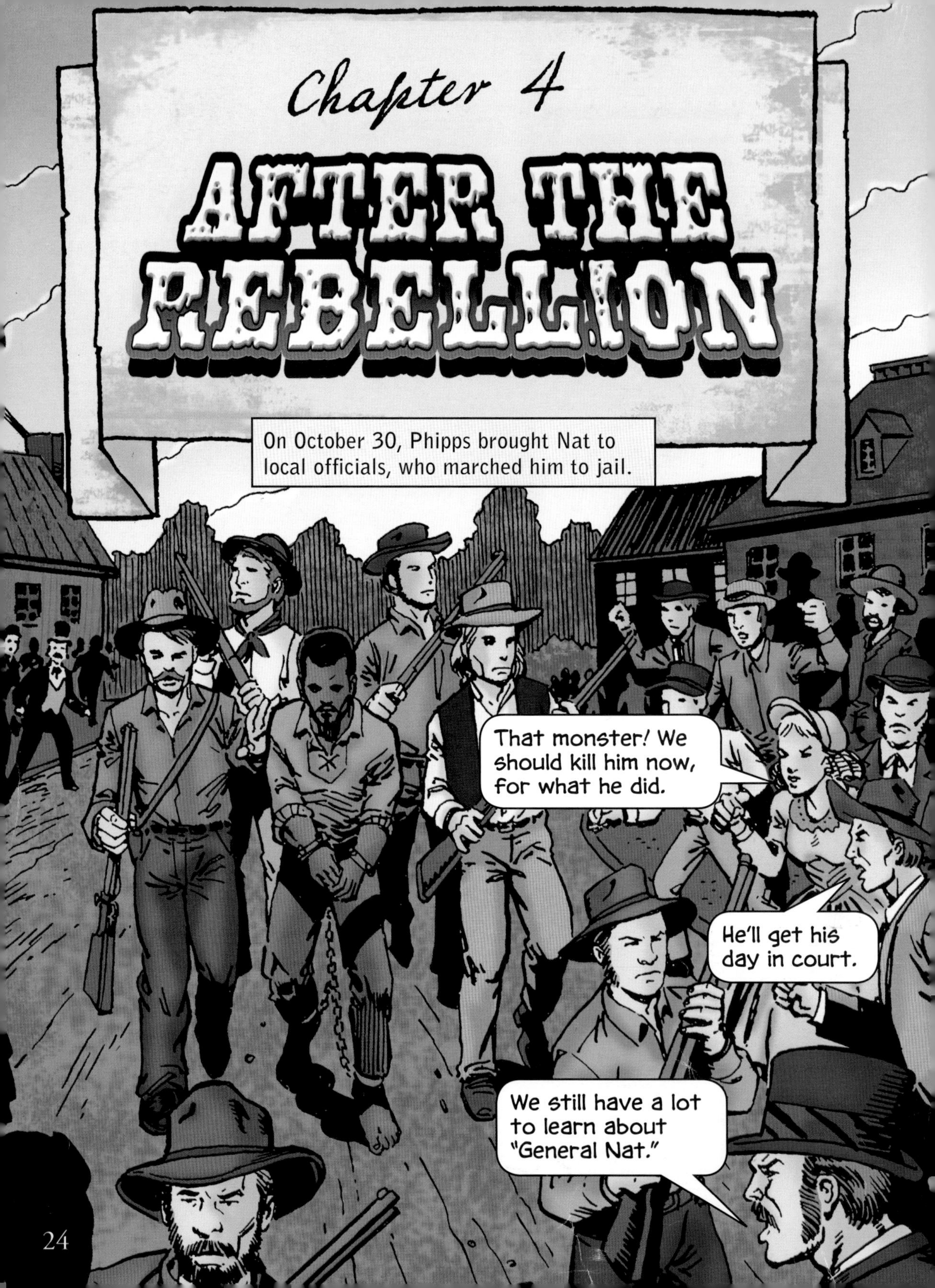

Chapter 4
AFTER THE REBELLION

On October 30, Phipps brought Nat to local officials, who marched him to jail.

That monster! We should kill him now, for what he did.

He'll get his day in court.

We still have a lot to learn about "General Nat."

NAT TURNER'S SLAVE REBELLION

Nat Turner was born October 2, 1800. After Nat's birth, his mother, Nancy, considered killing her son to spare him a life of slavery.

At the start of Nat's rebellion, Southampton County had a population of just over 16,000. Almost half of these people were slaves.

Many slaves protected their owners during the rebellion. At one house, a slave stuffed a cloth in the mouth of a crying child so the rebel slaves would not know where the family was hiding.

Some people feared that Nat's rebellion would spread into North Carolina. The people of that state did not have proof that their slaves would rebel. Still, some people killed innocent slaves.

Officials in Norfolk, Virginia, asked the U.S. military to help fight Nat and his men. Marines and sailors were sent to Southampton County, but the rebellion had ended by the time they arrived.

The $500 reward offered for capturing Nat would be equal to just over $10,000 today.

During the trials, a slave girl named Beck said that she had heard some slaves talking about killing their masters months before Nat's rebellion. Several slaves who lived outside of Southampton County were convicted because of what Beck said. The men said they were innocent, and many people doubted Beck's claims.

Thomas Gray published *The Confessions of Nat Turner* soon after Nat was hanged. Printed and sold as a pamphlet, Gray's *The Confessions of Nat Turner* gives a detailed account of the rebellion. Historians, however, doubt the accuracy of Gray's account. They believe Gray used his own words, not Nat's, to tell about the rebellion.

GLOSSARY

abolitionist (ab-uh-LISH-uh-nist)—a person who worked to end slavery before the Civil War

eclipse (e-KLIPS)—when the moon comes between the sun and the earth so that all or part of the sun's light is blocked out

militia (muh-LISH-uh)—a group of civilians who form an army during emergencies

preach (PREECH)—to give a religious talk to people, especially during a church service

prophet (PROF-it)—someone who claims to speak for God

vision (VIZH-uhn)—a dream that conveys a message

INTERNET SITES

FactHound offers a safe, fun way to find Internet sites related to this book. All of the sites on FactHound have been researched by our staff.

Here's how:

1. Visit *www.facthound.com*
2. Type in this special code **0736854908** for age-appropriate sites. Or enter a search word related to this book for a more general search.
3. Click on the **Fetch It** button.

FactHound will fetch the best sites for you!

READ MORE

Bisson, Terry. *Nat Turner: Slave Revolt Leader.*
Black Americans of Achievement. Philadelphia: Chelsea
House, 2005.

De Capua, Sarah. *Abolitionists: A Force for Change.* Journey
to Freedom. Chanhassen, Minn.: Child's World, 2003.

Gregson, Susan R. *Nat Turner: Rebellious Slave.* Let
Freedom Ring. Mankato, Minn.: Capstone Press 2003.

Isaacs, Sally Senzell. *Life on a Southern Plantation.* Picture
the Past. Chicago: Heinemann, 2001.

BIBLIOGRAPHY

Documenting the American South. *The Confessions of Nat
Turner.* (http://docsouth.unc.edu/turner/turner.html).

Greenberg, Kenneth S. *Nat Turner: A Slave Rebellion in
History and Memory.* New York: Oxford University
Press, 2003.

Oates, Stephen B. *The Fires of Jubilee: Nat Turner's Fierce
Rebellion.* New York: Harper & Row, 1975.

Tragle, Henry Irving. *The Southampton Slave Revolt of
1831.* New York: Vintage Books, 1973.

INDEX